The Recreation of Night

TAMARA FULCHER

The Recreation of Night

Shearsman Books
Exeter

Published in the United Kingdom in 2008 by
Shearsman Books Ltd
58 Velwell Road
Exeter EX4 4LD

www.shearsman.com

ISBN 978-1-905700-58-5

Acknowledgements:
Some of these poems have previously appeared, or will appear, in the following
magazines: *Chapman, Erbacce, Open Wide, Poetry Review, The Red Wheelbarrow, Shearsman,
Tears in the Fence.* My thanks to the editors for their support. 'In Passing' was featured
on the *Poetry Review* website in January 2007.

Contents

For Beau
sine qua non

O

He wants to root himself in my earth.

His root is pale, opaque,
the blind searching for the invisible
and for the nourishment of years
of death, decay;
searching through all my years, my earth,
their earth, their ashes, all their dust.
It seeks the water sprung
limed and rock-filtered from the core,
my core, the core of me.
We are indivisible, by his wish,
as air from the earth it smothers,
water from the earth it drowns.
We are one and together, we are one
in two, we are organic, we eat
each other.
Day, night passes, we grow into
pieces of ourselves, falling off
ourselves, our skin sheds, it is all
our earth, his earth, mine.

He wants to root himself in my earth.

His tongue is his eyes is his hand
and white in the way of paper,
still seeking, always, a flick
(err) of life in the woods, in the dark,
like a match lit and extinguished,
like the yurl of the fox

hunting and hiding.
I am post. I stand for
piss and acid air and knives
to scrawl over me. He wants
part of it, the flesh part,
the cut earth where
there is standing water,
the third part of it. He is opposite
in sense and physicality, and
in constellations. We look down,
his root is watching and it knows
it needs earth. Any earth. Warm
earth. My earth. My earth is
his dust.

He wants to root himself in my earth.

It continues. Pale and agape
mouth dry under our silence
and the watch of the owl who
mutters. The water is black
and bitter and grains float in it like
clots of mud, or blood, black and
sweet to swallow. The root has to hide.
It scours and ploughs a furrow in my skin,
my fur, as if it should have fur.
It has none. It has nothing but blood,
its face is blooded. At night I hear
the suckling cubs and the beak of the owl
tearing blood out of flesh and swallowing

bones like white splinters of wood.
It all passes through me
as earth through a worm, waste,
gestated and now fertile, now slick
with swallowed water.
What comes out of us is excrement
with a wet skin of skin, it is now earth,
it is ashes with the fire still inside,
white, it is the dust that circles
in the circling air, uplifted
into air, air to catch our eyes.

He has rooted himself in my earth.

(It is over. I faked it. The skin
the death
the water
it runs in, fills the hollow of me, runs away.)

There is no air.
Ashes are grey and among them are
broken things.
Earth is a circle
hollow and solid.
The owl dies too
the fox makes milk
white turns to black
with the small and sudden coming
of ink.

Air can turn to song
when he is inside

we grow
vines
in one another's hair.

ZEROED

I cannot quite believe it. Have just realised
the implication of your asserted statistics
and that they render me one unmatched half
for the rest of my living life.
Alone in a ball of utter squillions –
folk and molecules and pieces of air –
I will soon find a new inability to breathe
a sweet habit of looking at my toes
and a total corporeal dryness
that will never be dampened out.

You have are not divine but have divined
the road of my future,
the bend of its curve,
the up and away of my final fall.

CEREMONIAL

We begin at eight p.m., precisely, because between then
and quarter past we expect the small offering
from (always) a woman, wearing white or wearing blue
with (we know it, always) red inside, pushing her wood
on silver wheels before her with, perhaps, a shawl, wool,
over what she wears. We seat ourselves upon the floor
(no chairs but his) chewing cake we brought, which was
refused, our elbows on our knees, and after her the door
remains closed. The music is already playing, just loud
enough to hear cadence though not words, the way (he says)
he likes it. Then he comes. He wears a nightgown, dark
though not quite black, and brings a bell. The threads
of his hair shake as he nods and he says, 'You know,
my best years by far were playing under Louis XVI,'

and we agree. Then he reties his waist so tight it is beyond
accommodating the inhalation of air, surely, and asks,
'Have we had sufficient?' Throws his crown behind him,
opens up himself so we can see the purple of his mouth,
his throat, and swallows. Mother reaches to his cheek
and smiles; he rings at her, shows his teeth and turns.

I clear the plates and check for crumbs. He does not appreciate
remains, and has not eaten since a slice of seeded cake, which
left atoms of itself between the clean ridges of his gums. It had
not actually been brought for him, and on that nightwe had
already wrapped the knives, and left.

Ms Spring

. . . your face looks fine."

(and amazing
considering you've fed it for fifty-two years
on unfine white wine
so
I guess it must be genetic
and how greedily I want it

looking too long at your
(descended from Hungarian aristocracy)
silken nose
(maintaining their right to
anti-semitism)

wanting to touch it
wishing I had the blood
to take my drink)

PRECIOUS

Dressing yourself, you have found leopard-print tights
can be made to match a tiger-print top and ruby slippers,
absolutely flat; that you like yourself in denim only if
it has spurious stitching on the sleeves and something odd
about the collar, preferably something neon pink; that
you prefer to buy rings, laces and chains yourself, others
tending to base their choice on numbers of digits, price.
Down the road is your boyfriend, not three hundred yards.
You know that if you leave at 3 the navvies on the tarmac
will be packing up and looking for something live; that
if you wait until 5 all the sad fathers of all the angry kids
will be bringing out the dead – racks of lamb, chickens
separated from their feet – and looking for something,
anything with warm blood; that if you leave at 8
the car headlights coming on will shine right through you,
making your legs appear white, your shoulders wide,
your hair a buzzing halo of red – scarlet, actually, because
such a colour can be made to work, any time, any place,
in the right hands – and the drivers, all of them as if
processing, looking. So: some choices. It's a short walk
but you have all sorts of jewels to hang from yourself
and you do it slow without stupid, almost a dance.
It's only when you get to his house that his door opens
and the dark hurries in behind you, before you've even
seen it. Something he once told you: that a survey of
700,000 plus proved the no.1 point of male affection is
for the waist-hip ratio. That, he said, is science.
Just in case, you wear a plastic belt, though because you
prefer the theory of colours, display, you wear it amber,
because amber means Stop – No, Get Ready To Go.

Security
I am Security
I do not know

running a finger line
underneath his badge

(the woman had asked,
do you sell superglue?
and where would it be)

and thinking,
what I do with her is up to me what I do
with her is up to me what I do
with her is up to me what
I do with her is up
to me what I do

(there is always choice
but not always options)

we were in a room
appearing at first to have four sides
but on second looking
it did have six

walls
after all
do not protect from sun and rain
or from things that might emerge
from the earth

so I was picked
to deal with light

I chose electric
firelight
and I chose back
turn back
turn so our backs
are to the light

as you spotted the walls
above and below
decided to follow me
only with your eyes

because of the shadow
looming shadow
that our selves had struck

DIGRESS

Two doors, wood with woodworm holes
and snibs that do not fit, a floor
with old and older nails, and warping,
cracks through which we see the dead
lead pipes and wiring, human hair and
other grey shed bits, pulls from wool
and biscuit spills, then the silent sound
of soles as there you walk and there you

wait, small, before my door, your hands
about your waist and your bare back
sensing cold against the wall, you think
your nails need cutting and are here

to ask, for I have scissors silver sharp
and dull as self; for I know well how
to kindly wield if not to strike a hold,
and you sit straight as upright while
I snip, twenty times or more, and parts
of you begin to fall, mediocre white
into the warmer valleys at our feet.

With Thanks for Maxine Kumin

OH. My
fucking God
       (I love your aggression)

you are so good! Better than her! I know you talked
and that everyone wasn't interested and I know she talked
and you listened and that everyone was interested especially
when she put on that fur and gassed herself dead and that everyone
asked you for a response and you said, If you'd only listen,
       and that

everyone reached for her papers and remains

(and I found you on a shelf in a book called Jack which I only
picked up because a man called Jack once caught my eye
and I wished he hadn't and thought later that I might
buy him your book for his 42nd birthday and that
something else I knew was that you took
classes that it wasn't therapeutic)

now I have found you and you are so!
fucking good God
I want to grow you
like a seed

FACE

I
the first man I ever wanted to
do things to me

I was eight years old
watching TV
and the thought of it made me
sad

II
twenty-one years older
his hair is darker
my hair is darker
he is still on TV and
I still want him to do things
to me (kinda)
because he still has it

and the ugliest thing about him
is his jeans

III
he says he needs a prop
(I don't do props, except perhaps
white underwear, if
I have some already)
and doesn't like groups

(me too
how I want you
to drive at me through
the glass
in your big black
van, run me down)

CHOIRSINGER

My father said, So what do you do?
I stopped, and replied, I sing I the choir.

Choir? said Mother, That must take some work.
I said, It takes a lot,

and practice. He flicked his ash
into the hearth and I tried to stand taller.
It fell as small snow. My shoes were tight.
Do you perform?
Not on my own, Ma, I said, But we do.
Who?
The choir. We are many. She dropped her head
as he made a noise.
Outside was getting in, between the drapes.

I wish you'd told us, she said,
we'd like to have known before now.
The fire cracked. He made the noise again,
looking down.
We could have come to watch.
You can still come, I said, eager as a boy.

Oh, I don't know. He could still speak
to throw me off. He sucked on the end of it,
chucked it in to burn. It's a bit late for that now.
Season's nearly over, eh.
There is no season, I said. There is no season,
Mother said, pushing in,
it's all the time. He rubbed his red hands fast.

Oh well, he said, You'll let us know how
you're getting along.
What do you sing? she said, craning up.
Oh, I said, Just songs. Everything.
Yes, we said, Yes. He was still looking
down at the wood, white, shaking into air
and fading out of sight, out of being.
I saw her eyes were closed.

MOUTH

Perfect, except for one missing tooth
which appears black as absence
when you speak.

Your lips pull taut and slacken.
I think how their pink might feel
against my skin; how proper
it would seem against my white
or even the brown of down there.

There is that gap. Too big
for catching food or hair,
too much the wrong side
for whistling.

I think how its kiss might feel,
how tight the string of its purse would pull
and how utterly you might meet mine;
how I would fall right through.

AFTER THE FLOOD

This was her hair: as if a reach
had come and smeared it all with light;

and this was her hand: as if a sound
had curled itself in dust to fall asleep;

and this was her eye: as if a kind
had looked and she had looked at it right back.

Unfortunately, the most useful, the most exciting
fossils are complete skeletons, perhaps
with the remains of other skeletons
inside their bellies.

LIGHT POLLUTION

what should be cleaner
than the inside of a mind
but mine is not

you are in and stuck
like that wasp behind the shopfront glass
like that crust of chicken fat
stuck between the sinkhole spokes
too obscene to rescue

you are in
and it might be night above us both
but the city shines up its pink light
and stars cannot move to be seen

OF GAY ADULTERY

You had sex with Roger Moore.
Only once, you said,
while I enjoyed absentee hospitality at yours;
the scents of your waxed fruits,
flavours of your drinks.

You laughed that he used 'Me'
in the middle of his name,
his peacock display and mode of dirty talk;
something that struck, like how he never wore a suit,
while I leant, girl-drunk into your breeze.

A Primitive Truth

In actual fact she wasn't gagged.

Lucas had this thing, not to be
bitten but to have the girl pull back her lips to show
her teeth, for him to examine, and if
their white was white enough he would let her
slide it down his skin,
his notion being that she maintain constant contact
whatever snag, whatever trip her mouth might meet.

Matthias helped by holding her head.
He had all her hair, spilling through his fingers;
it made Marcus laugh and say, 'You look like you're
grooming a bitch,' but Matthias was thinking of his breathing,
the weight of a skull with brain and eyes, which hill and
how well her white was riding.

I called myself Jonas. She said, 'Like the whale?'
and I said, 'Mammalian, yes. But no. Jonas.' Lucas
though it was who hugged her, told her what to do and when
she might begin to think of stopping;

Marcus, inevitably, who said he'd heard that noise before,
he thought, in a zoo. 'The sound of a startled baboon,'
he concluded, and moved himself, to get a better purchase
on her end.

FILLING

Pizza. Pizza again
and not as cheese as the moon, but
a disc slapped out by a metal disc,
and white
until we heat it.
Then we eat.
We watch TV while it gets hot
and the white browns
and the cold goes,
then we watch TV
while we put it in our mouths.
Chew.
Chew once for sustenance
and once for comfort.
Chew until it is cold,
until it is white.
Chew.
We have its heat
and its shrink-wrapped
is in the bin.
It is gone
not round
but in a hole.
It is eclipsed
and our hunger is its umbra.

SARAH SAID, I LET YOU DOWN

I've done it twice now, haven't I.
Oh, don't worry about it, I replied,
feeling awkward, because I am,
also taller, and because
and my clothes are not
the gentle browns of hers
so that she looks like a piece of earth
and soft, as if she should be
in your hands.

My hands are empty. I look at them.
My hands are tied, Sarah said.
I smiled.
Something came up.
Did it. Did it
come up or come up
inside you, into
your serpentining heart, into
where I should be.
I did not speak.
My mouth is shut.

How Sarah's browns are gentle,
as if she should be earth.

SMALL IRRITATIONS WHILE FILM-WATCHING, I

A type of beetle, slim as my eyelash
rears its head between the corn-ears
of my finger hairs, spying
a descent. Too late. I can
make wind from mouth and shoot him
ass over carapace
back up my yellow-pink
and knuckled mountain, no need
to know whether or not
he died at the end.

SMALL IRRITATIONS WHILE FILM-WATCHING, II

We make it dark. We like it,
me to save my thighs and you
for your nails, to let them work.
Nothing quite like a jaggy clench
of flesh when neither expects, nor
your well-seasoned, three-digit stroke
of my shrunken second head.

Two-disc show. The lights are up
by your quick reach and I feel it
in my wetness, your watch as I come
between you and TV, touching DVD
playing at my toes.
And you have actually scratched me
so badly
that even my innocent hairs are split.

(Thirty-one seconds when everything we hear
is quiet: the slip and creak of my feet
moving on the boards – voices upstairs –
your nails, cutting their throats at your teeth.)

SMALL IRRITATIONS WHILE FILM-WATCHING, III

Shitforbrains: looking like you slipped your feet
into two quite clayey clods of earth, and like
you snagged your jeans conveniently
on six strategic nails, and like
you know not what to do
with curly hair;

shutthefuckup with your drum n' bass,
it doesn't suit my ceiling or the glorious climax
of *Repulsion*, when the sometime-boyfriend
is in her hall (having forced his way in
out of natural, sexual concern)
and she kills him.

oh man, and I think
what sin am I into now
what sin to conjure
the most grin

(I take his chest
and hit him there
for his lack of gloves
for his not looking)

it is to honour
my father and mother
that I must
and I must not

must love the sinner
must not love the sin

ON DEATH

The stink of its approach is
prickly and delightful.

It could all end with a housebreak
or a pre-dawn naked amble
down river, in the river;

or a monoxious hose,
his hand in mine.

I hope not. Hope is weak
and nothing stronger than hope.

I Don't Know Why

There are seeds in my baby's shit,
teardrop-shaped and squashable,
they turn into amorphous fibres
upon squeezing.

I don't know why this tiny man
is shitting kernels,
when he only eats milk
and the soft-sieved scrapings
of seedless things.

Unless he is passing pieces of himself
out to me
for safe-keeping.

you say you do not know
which part of me you
should eat first

there are so many
like warmed-through beans
or meaty sweets

nipples, clitoris, the
ends of all my fingers
and tip of my nose

I am just happy
to be licked
or to lick myself

I like the raw stuff

She is His Fantasy as He is Hers

I believe him that she thinks his penis is too small;
England makes its rock stars like rag dolls:
they might take some beating
but are not very good friends with eugenics.

He for one looks like back row third from the right
in the school photo;
wants to require more shaving than he does,
wants a good reason, for everything.

She at least don't need no reason.
She has planes, First Class and Mile High,
and with every slight crack in her line of sight
her bright lights higher.

You can imagine the two of them at it;
limbs chiming like silver spoons
and the mirrors, and the bruises after.
Then he'll sing something about white

and all the only-joking corners of the land,
as if they really were so funny to those
who can't afford to break everything they buy,
or even hearts,

and she'll look up at him as if she weren't really
looking down, wearing something in flamingo
and sincerely not smiling, letting us see
the thin twin clouds of her areolae beneath

and their life in pictures, hummed to a guitar
and holidayed in weedless shallows,
smoked out or at least kept up at night.
We watch them, dusting the corners.

MAN

You are behaving like a penis.
Quite literally:
big-headed and insistent.

You think you know
Truth.

All you really know is that you are
There
and you want to be
Here.

Somewhere you can see through
one eye half closed.

BLINDED

Hours, it is, at a time
between when you look at me
kind and smile.

Don't think I don't know
the scratches aren't by accident,
that I am the source of your
river tears.

I cry. You cry. I cannot stop.
Fondly when my hair is cut
and I try to stand up,
try to move your eyes.

I know too that you don't
want to see, to see me,
wall before you
and behind, that I am
your wall eye.

CLIMAX

The noise he made at the end
was like the slow and growing
start of an alarm.

I expected doors to open
by themselves,
the lights to cut
without a click.

He let go the air in his belly
and the smell of it spread like
rancid butter knifed
across the air.

At last I could stretch and leave.
He was smiling as if
I should be pleased as he,
unaware of how ugly were
the soles of his feet,
the back of his neck with its
unnecessary hair;

as if I should be grateful
for what just ended
in stink
before my eyes.

FIRELIT

(the orange of you is your best part
it makes me think warm at least
even on the first morning of october
when I cant smile like the rest
the silent others who can afford
to fill their lives with oil those who
watch tv as if it were written or dogma
who are parts of a recognisable whole
i have only you who listens when
i think i am greatful you sigh too
at the sounds i make in my sleep
your own name your light dims
with each shy autumn passing
on the rain we fade and as we do
oh beautiful how our shadows grow)

EWCM

Not much
is a matter of deserving
except, perhaps,
ribbon-hung medals for running
put about the necks
of those who run
like rope
to lift them up.

If I do not deserve it, then
I want it.
If I do not need it, then
I want it more.

Like him:
I take his two initials
and mix them with mine
to make a spell.
It is alchemy in flesh:
the gold runs down
my skin
and afterwards
I want to hang myself
from the beam of his looking.

where are a butterfly's bones

clippings of your hair
all over the kitchen floor

I swirl and swipe them up
into a handful
wherein a new crumb

furred pearl of you

(dreaming I show the baby
the butterfly asleep on the stair
and he murders it by grabbing

he could laugh
it probably goes to his mouth
I could stop it
or I could watch
to see what happens
when a baby eats a butterfly)

we roll on
heads between our knees

summer salt

where are you
again

ADULT'RESS

time and time again
I can't look him in the eye

he was my husband's best friend
Oh

the feel of that is better than
his cock inside
the time and time again
pull of his hands at my hair

and I turn over
I can
this way and that

he says I am
a fucking goddess
fancy –

does he mean a goddess fucking
or just a goddess in extremis

it started with a kiss and now it's this

he's bald
his eyes are set
mine looking down

at the first
one marked as mine and then

aborted
this one's not
my nails behind his balls

I can turn me over
I can turn away

A Dream of a Gun at the Temple of a Child

In all wars there are
tiny movements of tiny things:

the raising of an elbow which leads
the arm in an act of assent;

the finding of a roll of film
and its progress to the pocket
of a disuniformed slave;

the masking of eyes, the seeking
of ears in noise and the round
unresistance of a face.

This is my war, first,
and then ours.
The slash of bathwater, and then
its return to the pit of heat
between my legs;
its quick climb up the rungs
of your spine, its wave
up the back of your glee;
its spreading with a clear
like shadow, its movement
like blood taking the floor.

Of Suicide, Compelled

The legend needs that kick
like man needs fire;
a dive from the roof
of an eighty-five high
would never be enough.

It needs the cool catch of air,
body breaking with
the sound of landfill,
someone watching from above.

CATARACT

You are in my eye as if
a clot of cloud.

I can't see past you,
past your voice or how

you tend to buckle, the blackened
colour of your legs

or how you grow, how you
might as well be millions.

Despite that you sing flat,
dance out of tune, I am blind

for loving you. Under sunshine
we were made and fed and

under stars our nights will
fade together. Simple

as that I have you. He, She,
the light of their no purpose

sends me reeling. So does
the ugliness of white.

Should I reject disease when
it is part of me, or cherish,

salute a singularity?
I think so and know
that when you clear I will be
bereft, descarred,

made and visioned whole
as if a god.

CHILD, WATCHED

You are hot and newly shallow,
you like to lie on me to sleep.

Your ear has fluid in its craters,
the colour of straw.

You are all the colour of straw.

You have slept all day,
all night before it, and all this night too.
I wonder when I will start to cry
as you did, before,
when you were woken by the heat
for a sip of juice, or milk.

It is still night,
and there is always morning,
raising like a wail and white
in her church best.

Not like me. Not like me
cut at the knees and bound,
my hand to your head.
You are so hot, as I feel your water
rising to the cloud that made you,
taking with it all your colour
and all the music of your mouth.

NOSTALGIA GIVES ME TUMOURS

God, it feels like a satsuma stuck behind my solar plexus,
and the only thing to shift it would be a long thick doobie
smoked leaning out of a winter window
on the thirteenth floor.

I think of the times we laughed.
Once, when you came in from a bath
and asked me what was so great
about watching two poofs buy a house.
I loved you for exactly two minutes twenty after that.

And the things I used to say, begging you to keep it hard
when I knew I was fat, and that you hate fat,
and that it was the middle of the day so I couldn't even
hide it;
begging you to spray my face.

I should have known it wouldn't last
from the first, the time you told me you liked white suspenders.
Or from the first time I heard you pick a crap line
from a film script, and call it profound.
Or when you missed the point of the beginning of
Cliffhanger, which is not – as you thought –
Rambo's sense of guilt,
but that the girl was not ready to die.

But rather than try to wipe my mind with smoke
I should just remember all the times I beat your arse at poker.
When I was slim and you were soft,
when you fell asleep with your face in my cunt,
the time you shat the bed.

Make the satsuma shrink as though
the juice had been sucked out,
feel its skin slip sadly down my spine.

PINK

for Annette Lynn Selix

pick the best time

it could have been zero
when out you squeezed
wet and sore-eyed from blindness

or two
when you thought to talk
or (you imagined) eighteen
with grown-up breasts
and so many pink clothes to choose from
you chose them all
bra like a light veil across your
small hills of skin
pink shoes that disappeared your toes
something Barbie-esque between
you chose it in your head
already thought it to yourself

and maybe this will be your last thought
since you know a bit about
what eighteen year-olds can do
from friends who know more and from
your mother's inadvertent frown
you truly believe they do it
not have it done to them

and you only eleven

best or worst of times
this is the end of yours
and you have no real pink
except the inside skin
he makes you show

(at eighteen you would have known
the skin on lips is thin
which makes it dark and pink and
infinitely tearable
little more than membrane it splits
with just the slightest sly of cold)
at eleven you find out how

lips torn from gums
gums cut from teeth
teeth knocked from jaw
jaw broken
bent at the knees
(eighteen, and you would have done it prettily
not)
arched like a
kicked and damaged cat
breathing through your mouth
and thinking of a scream
thinking Mother
thinking Where is hearing
when you need to be heard
thinking as a scream thinks
it will never end

(at eighteen you would have bent
and thought about your nails
and that if he gets it right
this could mark the start
of the best
the best best time)
eleven
you don't know all of what it's for
or didn't
except not deliberately touching
except for keeping clean

and that's your problem
he likes it clean
not
(eighteen's been all kinds of places)
that he can have it more than once
he can't
and eleven has a voice
to speak with

he hears you
knows as well as pink
you ask questions of teacher
think about God and Love
and that this big thinking
(more than ever at eighteen)
thinks that This is Wrong
and knows
knows not yet he has to finish.

knows not yet that finish is wet
and a palpitating smash
a tipping over of eleven-ness
a high shining forehead hitting rocks
and breaking like a small
white and plastic toy with thick insides

you will think of him
behind you
watching you go over

it takes more than a second

(all those seconds that could have
made you eighteen
tens of hundreds of thousands of them
growing like hairs
upon your sliding legs)

should not have said
put your fucking eyes away
you pair of beasts
wanting like a beast wants fur
I am sick of your wanting
and your wanting makes me sick

(should have said
come to me
my hands were made for holding

you have paws that cannot grasp
anything but filth
and I will wash them
kneel and wash them
until we all are clean)

The Influx of Poles

When someone says 'Warsaw'
I think of uprising.

Three days ago I drove
to a warehouse to collect a parcel,
and the man who brought it out
had his picture in the dictionary
under 'swarthy'.

(I have also been
eyed
by two men, by a river,
when I was nearly by myself,
and they spoke so I could hear
because I could not understand.)

Back to the warehouse.
He said, "Sign; print,"
meaning my name,
then he pushed the parcel
over to me, and said,
"Nice day,"
as he walked away.

It's no longer done
to call them Fucking Gypsies
though Swarthy had those shoulders
that could surely lift a cart,
and that I think I'd like to breed with,
if only I didn't have quite so much money;

and by the river would have been
quite OK by me,
if only they had known
how to ask.

ASLEEP ON THE SOFA AT GRANDDAD'S HOUSE

Weird recollections. How the gloom when a bulb failed
scared the toes off of me. How my cousin's rubber collection
(I mean rubber as in eraser, though he probably had one of
       those too,
being peculiar) smelled so sweet, and my tiny-headed jealousy
not yet taught that green was wrong, and how I stole one
and then put it back. How I fell on my knees and was dragged
across a playground, so that the skin came away and showed
the yellow glue beneath, with bits of grit stuck to it, and how
my mother asked, Why did the other girl keep running?
She had the age, you see, and logic to ask why one child who was
dragging another child along the ground would not stop running.
We do not work like that which she failed to comprehend.

Then how I made my dreams badder by making up voices,
Ishbel and someone else, which I must have prised directly
from a book, seeing as how no-one's been called Ishbel
since 1932. And how I invented the death of a piebald gelding,
and cried about it to girls, to make them like me.
And how I seriously thought my mother was coming at me
in the evening, with a knife, having caught me with a friend
in her private bathroom, which was painted green and dusty.

In your sleep you cry like something caught and snot jerks
noises from your nose. How I was ten and watched all the
Freddy Kruegers with my gran, and wasn't scared, the Creepshows
too, which I only later learned were Stephen King.
All these horrors coming out of single figures;
the weird cousin showing me his cock when no-one else was in
and me telling nobody, ever, anything but lies.

There you sleep on the velvet sofa, shit brown with death grey
       polkadots
(the sofa, not you, you are jaundiced to a newborn tan and
       your shit
smells of peaches, and I adore you); there you sleep and now
       and then
your hands startle. I wonder at the clouds you try to grasp.

BABY

I dreamt that you were ugly
and woke with panic sucking at my breast
like a hungry child.

That I was wiping milk out of your hair,
and that your nose had grown too wide.

That you were wearing
clothes as tight as Superman's
and that beneath you'd grown
from some slim wisp of love
into a hulk, with biceps
harder than your head.

I cleaned your face
and gently closed your mouth.

Told you it was you I still adored.

Love, being underemployed (I)

every two or three years
you and I have one long
and significant conversation

and it is like standing for a long
and significant time
in bright sunshine

energising

and I do not think
nor have to
for I know I have you

(see you in 2009)

LOVE, BEING UNDEREMPLOYED (II)

if you were
something
I had worked on for a long
and lonely time

and I were an alchemist

that is how much I want
to put you
between my teeth

Love, being underemployed (III)

There are a number of things you have
and need to do
in order to get the best (me)
for you
out of this life (yours and ours).

One, is stop reading Charles Bukowski;
two, is start stalking me, because
I would respond to an obsession; and
three, is book three tickets to Sydney,
Australia.

I have an uncle there, and I would
play with you under a blanket
all the way on the plane.

Night, Whoring (I)

He had a good room. Probably
the best; a suite with a waist
(twin unnecessary doors), one
long and carpeted step, Georgian
window, view to the west
along the road aisle of city centre,
uplit with wet
reflections of streetlights
I wore them on my back

        he put the glass against my back
        and fucked me,
        cock and core at precisely
        windowsill level

liked me in orange and black

NIGHT, WHORING (II)

Slopful as a bucket of retch
your pink pissing finger gripped
between your dirty others
and oozing glue, a leak
that could be plugstopped by one
thick pin
to leave me breathing, leave
me free, leave me free
to leave

        but you puking on my belly
        sending a second upspray at my face
        the powder drying at an eyelash
        eyebrow hair one two three
        flakes of it in my crows feet
        flaking off

and I wait until you turn away
something you reach for
a look to the wall

before I wipe it
decrust it with two expired fingernails –
index, then little – until I am clean
as clean enough and you have folded
drying wormlike and dewarming
from your hub, past the hub of me
and both of us whirring down
all of you into mindful absentness
myself into flippant infinity

Night, Whoring (III)

Everything is reduced.
They call it a bath
                and sneer
when I wash it in a sink

(she advised me to carry
feminine wipes
and I asked, in my pretty pink
greenness, What for?)

Sleep and remembrance,
mostly,
the antiseptic quality
of spit.

No Meet Today

(from the top deck of a bus)

Today
through the glass of the bar
I saw your back
bent
form over form

(and the bus ran past
me like a jockey riding its jumps)

Her daughter died on December 15,
she wrote nasty films in her head and
sometimes wrote them down, let
her ex keep his bike in her spare room
when he was around, wore her hair
in curlicues and flicks across her face
and liked to check the percentage of pork
present in pork sausages before
she risked a purchase, and had only
just been thinking how it wasn't even
particularly cold, or even wet, that year,

and very shortly afterwards she went
to a cupboard and pulled out all
the packets, tampons, travel toothpaste,
ibuprofen, but there wasn't enough of
anything, and she regretted spending
money on that coat, it was in the sale
but still, £275 on a coat was obscene,
and then it was that her legs fell, that
her socks slipped and let her legs fall,
and that she thought of a new scene
for her horror: a man on the phone,
a man with a beard and a child, the man
with one hand over the child's mouth,
its mother trying to listen, hearing only
silence from the other end, and crying.

Ex

You have him won.
Like a poor trophy I will smile
as I pass him on,
still gleaming with my spit
and rubbed to a white shine.

He is all yours.
He and the sweated empty sheets
we rolled as new blue skin
around ourselves;
he and the afternoon, waking up
at two to fuck and
always to eat afterwards.

Can you always eat afterwards?
Can you wear your long and blonde
while your feet stand
in a pool of his leakings?
His water, it burns
like his ragged number one
will scar your cheek,
his dark cheek your neck
and thigh.

You know, he still feels warm.
Put your hand to his gut
and feel him alive. Feel his
coma tremor
as he breathes over you,
breathes your air.

You know, he is still breathing
from when he put
his quiet mouth on mine.

ORBIS

I see you – not sure if you know that
I see you
I see you even though I am too scared to
open my eyes

I see your light like fast light
like shooting the dark the
present time dead

that second that
splits into all
possible forevers

you are here. I know it. I know not
really who you are
except I feel I should
talk biblical
think with the respect you deserve

I see you when the lights are off or only
fifteen watts
rated for a baby and
my weak eyes my
human eyes
what are you now I ask
among other things
is it just a visitation
or more
an indication
vindication

our promise
greeting
exit sign

In Passing

We say a lot about
what we should have said.

Paper flies between us;
I choose you flowers, and
you tell me you're a man.

My reply is sensibility,
sometimes feeling like an
avocado pear.

Stoned. Two takes
of my hand; the press
on your mouth; the well
of your fist; our mutual
moving away.

PHOTOGRAPH OF ANNE SEXTON

You sit in your portrait
seemingly pleased,
talking aside but like your cheek knows
there is a man
looking with a lens.

Your dress looks like silk, eaten up
by orange holes at your breast, your waist,
your thigh, and pretty.
Your fingers are long and they speak
louder than you do,
a foot before your face.

I am surprised that it is clearly
1960-something,
I see the years in your hair,
the turn of your ankle and your legs
neatly crossed,
the way you brushed it, your
exterior décor,
you look nice.

Not sure if you wanted to be heard
or seen by me.
I prefer the artist to the art, always have,
the stories of their lives
and how and how face-on they faced
their final deaths.
You teased yours out
like a fine curl of hair made straight:

not possible, and yet, inevitable,
with enough work. The work of years.
It was a mask, or all of it, a masque.
It was those hands with nails,
hair in your hands,
dress smoothed on,
torn off, shoes so lovely.
It was all you gave time to, all your days
nailed to the year with photographs
and words.
You bade and made us listen
and we did,
and then did not,
and then could not but.

Autumnal

Most days are waste;
pile up
need to be burned.

Ideas:

Circle them
with numerology.

Build a fire
that goes out.

Drive somewhere
and stay in the car.

Not so easy to execute with a companion,
if he is turtle small
but skits like something shot.

Take him with you,
up and down.

He looks at you like
you have sight and magic.

Be together,
always.

Make the days
go away.

GAME

Five little prostitutes
jumping on the bed
one fell off
and bumped her head

(CRACK)

Mummy didn't call the doctor
but if she had
he would have said,

I don't do house-calls.

Four little prostitutes
jumping on the bed

(and the rest is history)

Mother, Come Down

I will be waiting by the chook shed in the mud.

I hear you are bay haired with grey,
walking on fours,
and age has milked your eyes.

Do not weep so silently.

I will lift your mane to rub your forehead clean,
to warm that point, crossed, between your eyes
where the bolt from the nozzle would go.

Your undreaming part:
its grease on my palm.

Forget the noise to which you shook.
Forget him and the new cold of September.
Forget his metal kick
and his defeat.

Walk by me. Or choose to walk behind.
I will lead you, two-handed and slow,
our wet heels sliding down the green,
with only the sigh of your emerald fade
to warm the dusk, to move
the stinking rain of night.

I will wear a rosary, like no other.
It is what you gave me.
Hail thee,
with a voice that loudens.

Join me as we toast the Christmas,
fat on mulled fruits and full of chaff.
The grass is dead as all our flesh.
Air cleaned.
Colour unspun.

Three years of yours make one of mine.

Two Ugly Carpet Fitters

It's been over a year now,
so don't be surprised,

and besides, I've always been fascinated
by men with unusual gaits, and you walked
as though unaware someone had nicked
your spacehopper. And you were blond, and curly,

unusual for me, but there you go. Refer
to the above. Anyway, I gave you the bigger
one, since you were clearly the apprentice,
stuck with fixing gripper around my toilet

and not allowed to handle cash. So I pulled
you in by it, and your boss is married,
I know because he told me. Actually he didn't,
but he did say, "We've got a 2 year-old, too,"

and I don't expect he meant him and you.
Regardless. Boss: you followed, kind of licking
your mouth and turning gay, a little,
opportunistically of course, and I became

suddenly ambidextrous with your
tracksuit ties and shirtholes, and pretty soon
I was roasting. Less a desperate housewife
than a hard-legged bronze, feeling altruistic

and I have Buttermilk on my bathroom floor
and number 80753/9 in the kitchen,

I have it all ways and more, I tip 20%
even though your hammering knocks chips

out of my white skirting, even though you
hammered the screws into the doorbar, while
I watched, and I'll tell you I was thinking,
"Is that what they call a Glasgow screwdriver?"

but never said it. Too busy not making eyes
at married Boss and listening to you
singing to each other upstairs, and going
red, and not liking the vinyl after all,

so that when you'd waved from the door,
Blond, kind of sarcastic because I didn't tip
at all, not even enough for a pint on the
drive home, so that when you'd bounced

(always bouncing) away down the hall
I got my hammer and I got my knife and I
cut it all out, cut the hide from the skin
and black-bagged it up, this went on just

most of the night and here I am,
two months later, nobody's been in
since you, and Boss, you weren't so awful,
a bit on the short side but I know what

I've heard about that, and Blond was surely
ugly but you all look the same with my

eyes closed, so I left the chips to make me
think of you, in the afternoons.

It's been more than a year now,
riding my hand.

Printed in the United Kingdom
by Lightning Source UK Ltd.
126021UK00001B/130-150/A

9 781905 700585